Elegy & April

poems by

Jesse Curran

Finishing Line Press
Georgetown, Kentucky

Elegy & April

*For D
husband, lover, friend
planter of fruit trees
companion
through the seasons*

Copyright © 2019 by Jesse Curran
ISBN 978-1-63534-854-5 First Edition
All rights reserved under International and Pan-American Copyright Conventions. No part of this book may be reproduced in any manner whatsoever without written permission from the publisher, except in the case of brief quotations embodied in critical articles and reviews.

ACKNOWLEDGMENTS

"April & Elegy," in *Ruminate*. Issue 43. Summer 2017.
"Dear Baby, Perhaps, Conceived" in *Cactus Heart*. Vol 12.5. 2015.
"Graduate School, Day Two" in *Spillway*. Vol. 23. June 2015.
"Fuji-san" in *The Common Ground Review*. Vol. 16. Issue 1. 2014.
"On Naming" in *Blueline*. Vol. XXXIV. 2014.
"Sustainability Studies" in *Green Humanities*. Inaugural Issue. 2014.
"Just Like This," "The Waiting Room at St. Catherine's of Siena," and "The Twenty-Third of August (After Yeats)" were recipients of the Dorothy Sargent Rosenberg Memorial Prize, 2013 and were published online.

Publisher: Leah Maines
Editor: Christen Kincaid
Cover Art: Jesse Curran
Author Photo: Dylan Licopoli
Cover Design: Leah Huete

Printed in the USA on acid-free paper.
Order online: www.finishinglinepress.com
　　　　　also available on amazon.com

Author inquiries and mail orders:
Finishing Line Press
P. O. Box 1626
Georgetown, Kentucky 40324
U. S. A.

Table of Contents

Elegy

Sustainability Studies 1
Late Winter 2
The Waiting Room at St. Catherine's of Siena 3
Palm Sunday 4
Spy Wednesday 5
Holy Thursday 6
Good Friday 7
April & Elegy 8
The Writer's Reason 9
9th and 56th 10
Alienation by Transcendence 11
Anatomy Scan 13
Fuji-San 15

April

The Closet Readers 17
Saratoga Springs 18
Return 19
Graduate School, Day Two 20
Allegro Sostenuto 21
Just Like This 22
Fourth of July 23
Ninth of July 24
Breathless Charm 26
Twenty-Third of August (After Yeats) 27
The Seventeenth of April 28
The Butterfly 30
Dear Baby, Perhaps, Conceived 32
Elegy & April 34

Elegy

Sustainability Studies

I've been trying to figure
where that feeling went.

Call it happiness or *joie di vivre*.
Name it the chartreuse promise
of unbridled self-invention.

Instead, the heart's rhythmic pulsing
its anxious insistence
and also the way it sometimes settles.

And so, this acceptance.

And so, a bit more cayenne on the tongue
the skin's blotched redness from his grazing stubble
shoes worn down by miles and days
just one leather bag for a lifetime.

Not the lion's freedom
but rather, the armored horseshoe crab
returning to the same jagged shore
for millions of years.

not inventing
just breathing

such questions

Is the world warming?
And what might that mean?

It is unusually mild this January
and last winter was the warmest
on record.

Late Winter

I spent all day staring out the window
searching for an image of tenderness.

In the kitchen, he slices onion and carrot.
He crushes garlic and dried cayenne.
He adds salt and stirs in the udon.
He makes a sharp soup for my stolid sinuses.

Sometimes tenderness is already inside.
And gratitude means giving up searching
outside.

The Waiting Room at St. Catherine's of Siena

No one wants to be here
though we find ourselves here
with a woman named Monica to the left
and another Monica waiting on the right.
Slowly, the surgeons emerge and say it went *well*.
I am waiting for a man named Herbie,
who has me or a taxi driver and a heart
so damaged that even the nurses wince and sigh.
In Siena, descending from the pastel *duomo*
Saint Catherine slipped on a step,
which is still marked with a cross.
In Siena, the marble is so soft and the city is so wrought
that it's no wonder she fell; maybe that day
Catherine was also in need of care.
Here, one of the Monicas tells me I'm an angel
because I'm decent and have the morning to spare.
And in surgery, Herbie finds no peace
not yet ready to die
still needing to grieve for his wife
who also fell down the stairs, twelve years ago.
Born into the Black Death, Catherine
was known for her letters, her mystical love
and for bringing the papacy back to Rome.
Catherine was a writer who could tell Herbie:
*It's time to let her go. None of us fare well, but we fare
aside one another.*
I have faith in cities like Siena
and in stories like Catherine's
and most of all in the baby carriers
that go in empty and leave full.
In the waiting room the universe exhales.
The newborns take their first breath
in the damp January air.

Palm Sunday

What configures grief?

Thunder in April?

Or knowing the strength wasn't there to plant the garden
knowing we should bury him under the tomatoes
knowing the Irish take the voyage back
across the open ocean.

The body weakens.
The man gasps for air.

This isn't about knowing.

Just this morning I was lingering
with the word *gasp*
though the gasp of wanting
a little dying
and not a lot.

As I searched etymology
you searched for air
in your final sleep
refining and defining
your last breath
while I
deepened
mine.

Spy Wednesday

Drab words for the funeral poem
despite the time of Holy Week
despite daffodil and hyacinth
and baby buds like powder puffs.

Only Wallace Stevens could make it sound good.

But it doesn't need to sound good
because you were good—good
beyond good.

Holy Thursday

I accept the bleeding willingly this month.
The pain in the body seems right.
Seems less than ever.
Seems to weaken the senses.
Seems the same
as your absence.

Good Friday

Thank the stars for mopping the floor
and midday Mozart. One week ago
you didn't wake. Don't make sense.
Rather, keep mopping. The mopping
is the only motion.
The spring struggles along.
Someone said it's *surreal*.
The blood rushes from the body.
The emptiness of almost everything.
Save love. Save making love.
Save longing and missing.
Save nothing. You saved
everything: seeds, washing machines
lawn mower engines, your communion
money. I spend everything
on flowers and restaurants
and trips to Trieste.
There is an earthquake in a medieval city.
Many die and more mourn.
There are also daffodils and snow flurries.
It is Holy Week, the promise of resurrection.
The Irish priest spoke of your tomatoes
and I wish we had buried you under them.

I brought you sunflowers.
You made me strong tea.

April & Elegy

I used to pray and sometimes kneel
and speak with the dead and think
they could hear me thinking. I was a child.
At another point, I believed in nature
and in spring to make us strong—
in healing through motion, magnolia,
and meadowlark. In the garage
your pansies were potted and re-potted,
telling me you were not yet ready to leave.
This is where the sense struggles.
This is where I go: to the pansies,
yellow and deep violet. Not consolation
but creation. Your funeral lilies
are heavy and white and teach
only fragrance.

The Writer's Reason

Like the white mold on the lemon
toward the bottom of the pile
so bright and so stinging
so suddenly soft, so surrounded—
cancer is often unthinkable.

I seek the steadiness of the stonemason,
his working hands unharmed by the rock.

The old sages say
what is most feared
is most what we need.

April is a month for falling in love.

January is the writer's reason.

There is no way to say
why or how or what we feel
only that we feel and are affected.

When I think of her in that hospice bed
I break
like the baby's glass bottle.

9th and 56th

there's nothing
that can warm this

save music and yellow
save a tiger lily
save forgetting

they sit
where they once
smashed plates

in wild love
in spring

this time
snow

the pallor
of their parting

not to say
it was bad

it broke

it needed

breaking

"Alienation by Transcendence"

A week ago, the red-winged blackbird poet
sang out and the anxious young student
heard the center of his singing. He said,
confuse the erotic with the spiritual.
She takes this with her, sits under the trees
working on making sense of history.
What she discerns is that hunger
is no longer hunger.

She sees how the poet doesn't age. His hair
long, crow black. His hands, so delicate.
And though he pleases her with the way
he speaks of birds being bound to land,
he disappoints the fat lady with too many
gold rings and too much purple eye makeup.
He sings of inflection and she thinks
of deixis. He sings of Jung and she recalls
Shakymuni. He says *Basho,* and she smiles,
yes, *Basho*. She sees how he cares
about the way that he breathes.

Following his reluctant instruction,
she goes outside and looks at a tree stump.
Sees it first as a surface for sex, a dais, a place
exposed for exposure. She looks longer.
Remembers making tortillas from leaves.
Filling them with wild blackberries.
Serving them on the stumps. Afraid they're poison.
Enthralled by their bleeding pigment. Not eating,
but feasting on summer. Deeper still, the rings
and the smolder. The crumbling bark.
The terror of compost. Whitman's skeleton
under her flip-flops.

She sees her days as fragments of eros.
Splinters of thanatos. Her godfather is dying.
Her best friends are pregnant.
The ice caps are melting.
The aureate light of early summer
fills the maples above. The chlorophyll
pulses. The firmament, a heady green cosmos.
She sits in a tree house, listening to birds.
Not knowing their difference. Always catching
their color.

For her, no divine beloved. Only a man
with dirt under his fingernails. Epicurus
in his spirit. She believes the words of a poet
might save a marriage. The red-winged
blackbird sings of the Tao, of archetypes,
metaphysics, transcendence—
and has, somehow—made her kinder
to her husband. Kindness
can save a marriage.

Anatomy Scan

waking to the headline: twelve killed
    in Paris magazine office
        fear polarizing people

here, this doubt, this peering in
    twenty-first century technology
        seeing beyond the senses

still so, when first I saw you
    I cried, next
        came laughter

the mouth opens and closes, vertebrae
    roll and flex, the four-chambered heart
        pulses, dark holes for the eyes

I knew then, that life
    with you, would be
        between us

that something was shifting
    a seeing into the senses, a sense
        of your distinct sense of self

next, eggs and bagels, dirty January snow
    after last night's hurtful words
        a quiet peace, your father

this man in front of me, is you, is here
    opening to me, ready to do anything
        for us, to be with us

yes, you're a blessing, reminding us
    to be grateful for the snow
        the silence

and most of all, your miraculous
    senses, your fully formed
        self

Fuji-san

Basho says to write like a knife
through a watermelon.

I say it's fine
to weep and hide.

To know the work is being still
is doing nothing, is failing.

For a week we sat and watched Fuji
waiting for the clouds to reveal her.

I wept in the station
and said words that hurt you.

We didn't make it to Kyoto
or see a rock garden.

We didn't eat sushi
or sleep in a ryokan.

We learned you like to ask for directions
while I long to find my way.

We drank coffee in the hotel room
in Tokyo, in morning.

In the airport you watched me leave
from behind thick glass.

And when you finally got home
you slept on the floor for days.

And I was so glad
to see you.

April

The Closest Readers

I listen to the philosophers use language
and when I enter words with them, I feel naked.
One young man who flares careful genius
tells me of the ancient temples of Siracusa.
Last time we spoke, it was the Bavarian black woods
and this time, in a flash of nothing or forever,
I see us there in leather sandals and rough linen
praying to our pagan past.
Naked and speaking, nakedly speaking
one sees deep time in his eyes and their reaches.
But then, Lacan, *paternal*, Lacan, *political*.

Once, I had a week in Sardinia
where I found a silver ring
and watched my reality drown
in the turquoise sea, in flesh,
in capacity.

O how the philosophers
seem to forget
the tanneries, the twilight
the wedding rings
the fishermen.

Saratoga Springs

All that can be said
is the music is sex.
No simile or figure.
I want to say it was *that*.
Would it work the other way?
Is sex music? Maybe.
But not all music
and not that music
not all the time.
It needs lightning and rain
a classy hotel room
in a risking town
evergreens, mid-August
and a dress
Henry James would call
the democratization of elegance
bought off the rack
walked out of the store
and maybe then
music is sex
extended for hours
sunflower and rain
the core and collapse
dancing and lightning
still coming
song.

Return

return
to a love born in spring

home
to the sycamores in Central Park

falling
into autumn's radiance

scrub
my calloused feet

rinse
the long summer's sand

comb
my salted hair

dress me
in a warm wool sweater

feed me
what Greece could not give me

your freckled skin

Manhattan in October

Graduate School, Day Two

Oh, Derrida!
Adorno, Foucault, Blanchot…
Oh, Benjamin!

Legions of theorists, critics
circling and certain.
I'll walk through your museum.
Just give me Sunday morning
a cup of coffee with cream
and two eggs, sunny-side up.

Look, there's my mother—
beautiful in her bathrobe,
clipping coupons and teaching
the grace of sacred life.

Allegro Sostenuto

let the song that opens today
        be a Beethoven sonata

you are the cello and the piano
        sounds the universe

let the morning sun burn the river
        aflame and flood

the window with faith—faith
        even in love, even

in obsession and cruelty, slanting
        toward wholeness

a minute in and you are still the cello
        the dance, the heat comes

alas, let spring arrive—today
        you play piano

Just Like This

one winter day of your thirtieth year
you take a cup of tart tea
and not because it tastes good
but because it feels right
you suspect with such sipping
a mode for longevity

and perhaps in this same season
you mislay some old worry
then choose not to seek it
or miss it
or feel guilt
to have lost it

so marriage seems a possibility
and careers of last century
so another trip to Italy
just seems to make sense

you might arrive here

without psychotherapy
without breaking down
without breaking through

you might just arrive here

some call it happiness
others deem it the present

though you suppose it's
lemongrass
rose hip
hibiscus

maybe life
is just like this

Fourth of July

Two translations
of the *Tao te Ching*
in the beach bag.

Dear Mitchell. Darling Hamill.

And yesterday
was the season's
first cucumber. Such sweet
independence.

Ninth of July

At least this summer I can say
there were afternoons
to hear the blue jays screech
from maple to maple,
that even with thunder rolling
I still took my walk.
And that there was time to sleep
time for the quiet river of memory
and the imagistic comfort
of reverie.

I think of the poets I love
and know the work need not be
such struggle.
Rather, it is the letting go
of book launches in Brooklyn
of baby showers for acquaintances
and of the belief
that beauty
can be bought.

It is the words—or the ways
we gaping people need them
as we need rain in mid-summer
and to rest when the air holds us back
from moving forward.

I was born in the same town
as Walt Whitman.
In love with his spirit
I attempted to become a critic
shaping arguments
on the primacy of place.

Poetry has always touched
what is real.

This afternoon I left the library
and decided not to drive to the city.
I spent more time with the thunder—
with breathing the summer
deliberately.

The collar-bone spreads open
the lightning flashes over the bay
the yellow begonia turns her wrinkled leaves
toward the purple sky.

everything is hovering
everything is possible

sometimes arrival is so slight

I almost missed the blue-jay feather
standing straight up in the grass

an iridescent flash of indigo

what matters
was perched

beneath
the cob-webbed
clothesline.

Breathless Charm

He has the confidence
of one

who has devoted his life
to the calling.

She is his student.
She has none of it.

So he feeds her the words
when she can't find them.

She's singing
the way you look tonight

on a Sunday afternoon
in a safe space.

I can't help thinking
there's nothing

more lovely
than imperfect
singing.

Twenty-Third of August (After Yeats)

I don't know how to weave
a spider web—nor could I
but I am amazed and arrested
by the prism of light
glistening through one.

Seek what they sought;
the daily work is trusting
the voice already here.

This summer I taught myself
to love earwigs. I let myself
rest enough to listen, to hear
the bluegrass fiddler
bowing her heart
in my heart.

Today is the summer's fruition.

Come winter.
Come the loss of it all.

We still light the candles.
We nod our heads to the sun on the water.

Yes, we are blessed
and we bless.

The rickety back deck
is the lotus land.

The Seventeenth of April

Three weeks left of class. The old
crashing sounds. The sudden surfacings.
This term, with a potential promotion
looming, they seem even louder.
More precarious. A year ago, I was
three weeks away from eloping.
From Tuscany. This April, I'm feeling
far less lyrical. Teaching patient reading
in the virtual age. The students like videos.
They have become good at reminding me.
They are visual learners. A job-market
death sentence, I'll confess anyway:
I don't actually use technology
in the classroom. Nor do I want to.
Instead, the way a novel shapes
its own sense of time. How a poem
asks you to touch language, to find
its tenderness, graze its limits. More so,
the way this becomes a space for longing.
For memory of eros. Of music fleeing.
The realm of heady flesh. The open kingdom
of carnal consciousness. Remember
the professor you fell in love with. The knowing
it would never work. The being young.
The waiting for what might work.
It's memory trapped in lilacs. Vodka drinks.
His wing-tipped shoes. The way a book
can teach you to love the earth. To lay
your body close to it. Somehow a substitute
for the imagined, ever-distant lover.
Those dizzy lilacs mean graduation. Taking
the Van Gogh posters down from the walls.

Packing again. They mean moving forward.
Summer. The fearsome becoming. The future.
One of my students seems his generation's
beat-nick hipster and calls what he does
poeming. He tells me my class has him thinking
he should quit his job at Stop and Shop
for something more agricultural. My heart
goes out to all of them. Even the chatty Cathys.
Even the ones who lie about dying grandmothers
and broken mufflers. Three weeks left. Here,
at thirty-one, I keep trying to feel what I felt
at twenty-one. It was rapture. It was
what the beloved book says. Between fear
and sex. It was the very feeling that made me.
Brought me here. Gave me this memory.
This fire.

The Butterfly

> *I embrace emerging experience. / I participate in discovery*
> *I am a butterfly. / I am not a butterfly collector.*
> —William Stafford

When weariness of the world grows in me
I read some William Stafford, and then
I look more fondly on my failure.
I am a butterfly, not a butterfly collector.
And after reading one or two
of the twenty two thousand,
I can face the details of my days; days
as an adjunct in suburbia, asking
her students to ponder the planet's health
from this place, where so many seem
so very frazzled about what's coming.
Yes, I can face these ordinary days
and make poems that sound so simple
they seem to verge on self-help, on sentiment.
I don't mind being out of fashion.
The pen finds the page each evening, inspired
by the likes of poets past, poets
who crafted the practice first, and then
the line followed. The line follows
the splendor of the afternoon, my lover
making the autumn's first squash soup
while the ten thousand maple leaves
share the same earthen glow
as the butternut. I won't pretend
to find the words for them.
Instead, I'll sing their praises
and plant milkweed, fluttering
my wings and flying. Flying
even if, because, like the bees
the butterflies seem fewer these days.
To be human is to be humble.

To be humble is to surrender
to the steady flow of the breath
the certainty of the silence
this sense that there are
only these days
to revel in being
a ruby heliconius
born on the flesh
of a violet
passion flower.

Dear Baby, Perhaps, Conceived

Another new study posted on yet
another new web board. A mother's
diet at the moment of conception
can be determining. So, in case
one day you wonder, two nights ago
was chick peas, tomatoes, Indian
spices. Last night, your father, my
love, cut the garlic scapes. I made
pesto with lemon juice. We ate it
with pasta and broccoli. Then
we made love with our garlic breath
and our sweat was sweetly allium.
My dear, let me tell you how happy
we are. You see, we want you. We
patiently wait to see when you'll find us.
In the meantime, a banana, a handful
of almonds, the leeks pulled today
for tomorrow's cold soup. Don't forget
afternoon coffee with biscotti.
Let me tell how I love him. His walking
the earth. The dirt under his nails. His legs
like tree trunks. His ass, I tease, like
Adonis. The hundred fruit trees
he planted this spring. He plants them
for you. Yesterday, leaving the library
I browsed the new books, pulling
a name book. I open to witness
the first name of thousands. It was
the one we want for you. Leona,
Leonie. Tonight is June's full moon.
The rose moon. The honeymoon.
The strawberry moon. With haze
and rain, there's no pink to be seen.

My darling godfather, upstate
is in comfort care. My normal advice
is to breathe. With the tumor in his throat
and the trache, those words seem all wrong.
Impossible. For the waxing full, thick mist.
For the waning, a thunderstorm, smell
of worms rising from damp earth.
The sweet humid rot, the fruit flies
swarming the compost. Know
you are wanted. That we want you.
Know we would give you
this mystery.

Elegy & April

Most poems seem to come
from crying or from singing.
The thunder rumbles.
We are quietly waiting
for cicada song.

Jesse Curran is a poet, essayist, scholar, and educator who lives in Northport, NY. Her creative work has appeared in a number of literary journals including *Ruminate, About Place, Spillway, Leaping Clear, Green Humanities, Blueline,* and *Still Point Arts Quarterly.* She was the recipient of the Robert Frost Haiku Prize through the Studios of Key West (2013), a Pushcart Prize Nomination (2017), and an award from the Dorothy Sargent Rosenberg Poetry Prize (2013). Her scholarly criticism theorizes the regenerative relationships between contemplative pedagogy, ecological thought, and American poetry. She currently teaches at Stony Brook University, where she received her PhD in English. She is also a certified hatha yoga instructor and permaculture designer, two practices which inform her approach to education, sustainability, and community building. She is the mother of two bright stars, Leona and Valentine. For more about Jesse's work, visit her website: www.jesseleecurran.com

www.ingramcontent.com/pod-product-compliance
Lightning Source LLC
LaVergne TN
LVHW041600070426
835507LV00011B/1217